AF428725

To-Do-List

This Book Belongs To:

TO-DO LIST

I need to:

Done!

Notes:

TO-DO LIST

I need to:

Done!

Notes:

TO-DO LIST

I need to:

Done!

Notes:

TO-DO LIST

I need to:

Done!

Notes:

TO-DO LIST

I need to:

Done!

Notes:

TO-DO LIST

I need to:

Done!

Notes:

TO-DO LIST

I need to:

Done!

Notes:

TO-DO LIST

I need to:

Done!

Notes:

TO-DO LIST

I need to:

Done!

Notes:

TO-DO LIST

I need to:

Done!

Notes:

TO-DO LIST

I need to:

Done!

Notes:

TO-DO LIST

I need to:

Done!

Notes:

TO-DO LIST

I need to:

Done!

Notes:

TO-DO LIST

I need to:

Done!

Notes:

TO-DO LIST

I need to:

Done!

Notes:

TO-DO LIST

I need to:

Notes:

TO-DO LIST

I need to:

Done!

Notes:

TO-DO LIST

I need to:

Done!

Notes:

TO-DO LIST

I need to:

Done!

Notes:

TO-DO LIST

I need to:

Done!

Notes:

TO-DO LIST

I need to:

Done!

Notes:

TO-DO LIST

I need to:

Done!

Notes:

TO-DO LIST

I need to:

Done!

Notes:

TO-DO LIST

I need to:

Done!

Notes:

TO-DO LIST

I need to:

Done!

Notes:

TO-DO LIST

I need to:

Done!

Notes:

TO-DO LIST

I need to:

Done!

Notes:

TO-DO LIST

I need to:

Done!

Notes:

TO-DO LIST

I need to:

Done!

Notes:

TO-DO LIST

I need to:

Done!

Notes:

TO-DO LIST

I need to:

Done!

Notes:

TO-DO LIST

I need to:

Done!

Notes:

TO-DO LIST

I need to:

Done!

Notes:

TO-DO LIST

I need to:

Done!

Notes:

TO-DO LIST

I need to:

Done!

Notes:

TO-DO LIST

I need to:

Done!

Notes:

TO-DO LIST

I need to:

Done!

Notes:

TO-DO LIST

I need to:

Done!

TO-DO LIST

I need to:

Done!

Notes:

TO-DO LIST

I need to:

Done!

Notes:

TO-DO LIST

I need to:

Done!

Notes:

TO-DO LIST

I need to:

Done!

Notes:

TO-DO LIST

I need to:

Done!

Notes:

TO-DO LIST

I need to:

Done!

Notes:

TO-DO LIST

I need to:

Done!

Notes:

TO-DO LIST

I need to:

Done!

Notes:

TO-DO LIST

I need to:

Done!

Notes:

TO-DO LIST

I need to:

Done!

Notes:

TO-DO LIST

I need to:

Done!

Notes:

TO-DO LIST

I need to:

Done!

Notes:

TO-DO LIST

I need to:

Done!

Notes:

TO-DO LIST

I need to:

Done!

Notes:

TO-DO LIST

I need to:

Done!

Notes:

TO-DO LIST

I need to:

Done!

Notes:

TO-DO LIST

I need to:

Done!

Notes:

TO-DO LIST

I need to:

Done!

Notes:
____

____

TO-DO LIST

I need to:

Done!

Notes:

TO-DO LIST

I need to:

Done!

Notes:

TO-DO LIST

I need to:

Done!

Notes:

TO-DO LIST

I need to:

Done!

Notes:

TO-DO LIST

I need to:

Done!

Notes:

TO-DO LIST

I need to:

Done!

Notes:

TO-DO LIST

I need to:

Done!

Notes:

TO-DO LIST

I need to:

Done!

Notes:

TO-DO LIST

I need to:

Done!

Notes:

TO-DO LIST

I need to:

Done!

Notes:

TO-DO LIST

I need to:

Done!

Notes:

TO-DO LIST

I need to:

Done!

Notes:

TO-DO LIST

I need to:

Done!

Notes:

TO-DO LIST

I need to:

Done!

Notes:

TO-DO LIST

I need to:

Done!

Notes:

TO-DO LIST

I need to:

Done!

Notes:

TO-DO LIST

I need to:

Done!

Notes:

TO-DO LIST

I need to:

Done!

Notes:

TO-DO LIST

I need to:

Done!

Notes:

TO-DO LIST

I need to:

Done!

Notes:

TO-DO LIST

I need to:

Done!

Notes:

TO-DO LIST

I need to:

Done!

Notes:

TO-DO LIST

I need to:

Done!

Notes:

TO-DO LIST

I need to:

Done!

Notes:

TO-DO LIST

I need to:

Done!

Notes:

TO-DO LIST

I need to:

Done!

Notes:

TO-DO LIST

I need to:

Done!

Notes:

TO-DO LIST

I need to:

Done!

Notes:

TO-DO LIST

I need to:

Done!

Notes:

TO-DO LIST

I need to:

Done!

Notes:

TO-DO LIST

I need to:

Done!

Notes:

TO-DO LIST

I need to:

Done!

Notes:

TO-DO LIST

I need to:

Done!

Notes:

TO-DO LIST

I need to:

Done!

Notes:

TO-DO LIST

I need to:

Done!

Notes:

TO-DO LIST

I need to:

Done!

Notes:

TO-DO LIST

I need to:

Done!

Notes:

TO-DO LIST

I need to:

Done!

Notes:

TO-DO LIST

I need to:

Done!

Notes:

TO-DO LIST

I need to:

Done!

Notes:

TO-DO LIST

I need to:

Done!

Notes:

TO-DO LIST

I need to:

Done!

Notes:

TO-DO LIST

I need to:

Done!

Notes:

To-Do-List
Book Club